Remembrance of Lost Loves

REMEMBRANCE OF LOST LOVES

Poetry by

GENE JACKSON

iUniverse, Inc.
New York   Bloomington

REMEMBRANCE OF LOST LOVES

Copyright © 2009 by Gene Jackson

iUniverse books may be ordered through booksellers or by contacting:

iUniverse
1663 Liberty Drive
Bloomington, IN 47403
www.iuniverse.com
1-800-Authors (1-800-288-4677)

ISBN: 978-1-4401-9096-4 (pbk)
ISBN: 978-1-4401-9097-1 (ebk)

Printed in the United States of America

iUniverse rev. date: 11/18/2009

TO LOIS

Companion, friend and partner
And my love that has never been lost

CONTENTS

"I sit and meditate about the things I brought to Art,
Desires and feelings----some things half seen,
Faces or lines, some indistinct memories
Of unfulfilled loves. But let me rely on her.
She knows how to fashion a figure of beauty;
Almost imperceptibly rounding out life,
Combining impressions, combining the days."

from a translation of the modern Greek poetry of

Constantine Cavafy.

"This is for all ill-starred lovers
Unborn and unbegot,
For them to read when they're in trouble
And I am not."

from "A Shropshire Lad"

A.E. Houseman

THE COURSE OF LOVE

Young lovers often leave when love is finished,
Or when they find initial passion spent,
By this they mean desire is now diminished,
Their focused fancy was not permanent.

This fault is found in immature illusions
That love is simple, easy to achieve,
It leads them into deadly self-delusions
Which briefly they are able to believe.

This fatal flaw does not at first affect
The one who thinks of love as frivolous,
Or both the pair may equally neglect
To treat another's faith as serious.

But one who truly cares and is betrayed
Will be afflicted by a loss of trust,
For what seemed ardent proves a masquerade,
And love is led astray, becoming lust.

The fates, uneven, scatter pain and pleasures
In unfair random fashion out among
The ones who grow, adopting prudent measures,
And those who try to stay forever young.

Both you and I would give our lives to be
Considered faultless in this small charade
That occupies our early history,
And if resolved, will leave us unafraid.

If so, the adolescent must mature,
Be willing to renounce brief ecstasy,
Euphoria with all its false allure
Of hollow fun and false diversity.

Remember though, that balancing each loss
May be potentially a greater gain
For those who can cast off the albatross
Of cyclic paradise and lonely pain.

Achieving this requires experience
Not always easy, or a pleasant one,
But which, if followed through with diligence
Will bring us faith and love, in unison.

This is the story of one journey through
The exaltation and the misery
Which all of us encountered as we grew
From foolishness into maturity.

Occurrences I will describe are true,
Though some may seem to be a mere rehearsal;
The lessons that they taught were overdue,
And yet I do believe them universal.

You may dismiss them if you are inclined
To think of life and love as always static,
But if your passions are not well-defined,
Affection and regard remain erratic.

And those whose tenderness is superficial
Will never find a deeper love to share,
Devotion must develop past initial
Attraction and a very brief affair.

But if we find our way past foolish revels,
Apply ourselves to one ideal endeavor,
Then we will reach those deep far-reaching levels
Where trust and confidence exist together.

I. THE YOUNG MAN IN LOVE

"When I was one-and-twenty
I heard a wise man say,
'Give crowns and pounds and guineas
But not your heart away;
Give pearls away and rubies
But keep your fancy free;'
But I was one-and-twenty,
No use to talk to me."

A.E. Houseman

Tell the wind to come at your command,
Or send the evening star across the sky;
Find the source where truth and beauty lie,
And bring the night to cool the weary land.
The star will never stay within your hand,
The quiet air will silently go by,
And perfect beauty will escape your eye,
A fact the young refuse to understand.
But seek to love, and if your love be true,
Then truth itself the greatest gift shall send,
To share a part of that which will not die,
Know all the beauty that man ever knew;
Unbidden, night shall come upon the wind,
To fling her sentinels across the sky.

EARLY SPRING

I met you first in early spring
As winter's sterile state, retreating
Gave guarded sanction to a thing
That later proved to be so fleeting.

I should have been more cautious, waiting
Until initial passion waned,
Excitement may be stimulating,
But often cannot be sustained.

And so it was, I was to blame
For kindling fires that could not last,
The faintest breeze put out the flame
As soon as first desire was past.

Illusions are a fragile thing,
They lead you into faithless dreams,
Especially in early spring
When truth is never as it seems.

THE DOGWOOD TREE

I rode along a woodland trail to find
A fragile beauty of a certain kind,
Imagining the lacy filigree
Of springtime's brief and fleeting dogwood tree.

I found it hiding in the woods
Where shyly it would show its face
In isolated neighborhoods,
Exhibiting uncommon grace.

Appearing through the light and eager green
It was the purest white that I had seen,
And represented beauty that appeared
Before the waking forest interfered.

Its branches long and jeweled but
With empty spaces in between
Were flowing streamers still uncut
Like ribbons, pure and white, pristine.

Dismounting, I stood underneath
To see the branches like a wreath
Reach out, a ring around my head,
The garland of a girl, unwed.

Then standing close beneath the dogwood tree
I saw the lacy limbs among the green,
Withdrawing as they went away from me
And noticed there was nothing in between.

The flowers of the purest white
Had disappeared as if forbidden
To show themselves for my delight,
And so, retreating, now were hidden.

I came too near to have a fair perspective;
Detachment re-enforced my fantasy,
But scrutiny had proven this defective
And it dissolved into reality.

My love was like the distant dogwood tree,
I saw her once across a crowded room,
Her fragile beauty there for all to see
Amid champagne and laughter and perfume.

Admirers gathered to this shrine
Of beauty rich as vintage wine,
Attracted like the moths at night
Will circle near a brilliant light.

Her brief attention fell sequentially
On each whose turn would come and then would pass,
Her grace was constant, but fidelity
Was brittle as the wine-containing glass.

And I was part of her collection,
Amusing men she would select
To see a part of her affection,
While all the rest she would reject.

But even so I found that I became
Enamored, and revolved around her flame,
Some times so close her radiance might singe,
At others, relegated to the fringe.

A star within her constellation
Might alternate in dominance,
And flattered by her adoration
Not see its true irrelevance.

It took a certain distance to regain
A true perspective: I had loved in vain;
While laughing with another two or three,
She certainly did not have time for me.

And only then I realized
The fatal flaw in my affection,
The image that I idolized
Might prove to have an imperfection.

A Dresden figurine stood on a stand,
The likeness of my lady, so it seemed,
A graceful form with one extended hand,
Inviting all to share what I had dreamed.

It was at first across the room
Remote and isolated there,
An image which one might assume
Would be safe-guarded anywhere.

In its own space it stood alone
The very essence of perfection,
Inviolate upon the throne
That was its only true protection.

But then the crowd that swirled around
The flame that was my love extended,
It threatened to besiege, surround
The figure that was undefended.

I tried to call "Look out, beware,"
But then, before I could have spoken,
The lady lay beyond repair,
Her body permanently broken.

I seemed to be the only one distressed
At what this misadventure signified,
Before that moment I could not have guessed
The figurine was hollowed out inside.

I saw my fantasy disintegrate,
And wondered how it was that very little
Disorder was required to devastate
A work of art that proved to be so brittle.

The hostess only said, "Oh, well
It merely was a bagatelle,
And I can find another vase
To occupy that empty space."

They all were careless people, who could shatter
A sculpted figure or a naïve heart,
Pretending neither one would truly matter,
Their selfish world contained no counterpart.

Retreating into youth and carelessness,
They lived their lives untroubled and blasé,
And left to someone else their thoughtless mess;
So, sad and half in love, I went away.

I counted this a lesson learned,
Resolving never to repeat
Encounters that had only earned
A memory so bittersweet.

Do not approach too closely things you love,
Proximity may illustrate the flaw
That you have had no indication of,
And in your vain illusion never saw.

So, from a distance, like the evening star,
I will appreciate the dogwood tree,
Admire the figurine, but from afar,
And I will love again, but cautiously.

BORDERS

There is a place that I have known
With room enough for two,
But not available to one
And three would never do.

The borders of a young man's heart
Are rigid, fixed and brittle,
With too much strain they break apart,
Dissolving with too little.

My loneliness was commonplace,
And yet it did impel
A rash attempt to fill that space,
Succeeding all too well.

Instead of just myself and one
I added two and three,
What had in innocence begun
Would finish painfully.

So when you love, restrain desire
To what your heart can handle,
For passion, dangerous as fire
Can burn out, like a candle.

Before it dies, the flame can flare
To singe your heart and soul,
You pay a price in great despair
For loss of self-control.

Then, with these borders fragmentary,
An endless time is needed
To reconstruct a sanctuary
Like that you have conceded.

There is a refuge, light and airy,
A place that I have been,
Where one whose life is solitary
Can never go again.

LUDLOW FAIR

I knew you well not long ago,
I think it was last spring;
Our love, as far as I could know
Was endless, like a ring.

A ring is round in one dimension
But empty in another,
Seducing us to pay attention
To one and not the other.

Last spring is when it all began,
Commitment then was new;
Each time we met we seemed to plan
A secret rendezvous.

I still remember well the day
We went to Ludlow Fair,
And found the wonderland that they
Assembled on the square.

In spring the butterflies emerge
From all their secret places,
And at a certain time converge
To color barren spaces.

The splendor of their wings and back
In water-colored hues
Were brilliant orange veined with black
And lighter yellows, blues.

Our lives were then in parallel,
Two edges of the ring,
And went around, a carousel,
A whirling, gaudy thing.

Indeed, there was one at the fair,
Fantastic, exquisite,
With figures floating in midair,
Vivacious, brightly lit.

The carved and painted horses fled
Unhaltered through the night,
Like dreams that snatch us from our bed
And sweep us out of sight.

They surged, retreated, rose and fell
And circled endlessly,
So neither of us could foretell
The journey's brevity.

The whirl continued for a time
Through summer's endless days,
When nights were short but seemed sublime
In many magic ways.

A hurdy-gurdy filled the air
To match the carnival
So closely we were not aware
It was mechanical.

Our feelings and sensations mixed,
The elements all blended,
And spun into a swirl, unfixed
Until the music ended.

We felt the silence in the air,
The frozen carousel,
But I had silver still to spare,
And would not say farewell.

I paid the price to start again,
It came to life, and soon
The horses moved, but only when
They heard the gaudy tune.

A hoop was hung just out of reach
And swaying in the air,
There surely was some prize for each
Who caught it, dancing there.

While moving down and up, around,
I tried to seize the ring,
But with the swerving changes found
It was no easy thing.

Criss-crossing motion was erratic
Irregular, not parallel,
My efforts, although acrobatic,
Were countered by the carousel.

Commitment grants no second start,
No pathway to re-enter,
I missed the outer, endless part,
And held the empty center.

The time, I knew, would soon arrive
When I no longer could
Pay out to keep the fun alive,
And you found one who would.

He was quite handsome, I could see
And tall and strong and witty,
Who cared about integrity
When he could pay the kitty?

Our fates, distributed by lot
Are past all reckoning;
He had the luck that I had not,
So he had caught the ring.

A love allows some variations,
But not a fickle heart,
With one too many aberrations
The fabric falls apart.

The magic horses moved somehow
But creaked like un-oiled leather,
The carousel turned slower now
Then halted altogether.

The hurdy-gurdy sounds that matched
Our frivolous delight
Were weaker now, and often scratched,
No longer filled the night.

The autumn air was thin, austere,
Predicting winter weather,
And I would wake, that time of year
To frost upon the heather.

I went again to Ludlow town
To see where we had been,
The colors now were shades of brown,
And desolate the glen.

I looked once more into the square
Where butterflies had fluttered,
And even though it still was there
The carousel was shuttered.

For winter is the barren season
When all lives involute,
So certainly that was the reason
The music-box was mute.

Our love was like a fragile shell
That, richly decorated
Was beautiful if handled well,
But cracked when agitated.

I felt an odd emotion there
Which I had never known,
We two had gone to Ludlow fair,
And I came home alone.

So half-way round the cycle ran
From spring into the fall,
I knew you well when we began,
But later, not at all.

II. THE FAIR YOUNG LADY

"Oh, when I was in love with you,
Then I was clean and brave,
And miles around the wonder grew
How well I did behave.

But now the fancy passes by,
And nothing will remain,
And miles around they'll say that I
Am quite myself again."

A.E. Houseman

EVALUATION

Why should I tell my lady she is fair?
She knows as well as I that it is true,
For all who see her add their praises too,
Her beauty is for all the world to share.
Why should I also tell her of her rare
And graceful countenance as others do?
Of eyes like sunlight when the world was new,
Her face a star within her midnight hair.
No, I will look beyond and find her heart,
And tell her of its worth and of her grace
Of spirit and of mind, and all the while
Will hope that I may someday share a part
Of all her beauty, and within her face,
May touch the magic of her secret smile.

INVITATION

Would you come and lie with me
Upon a summer's sunny field,
And watch the day that we can see
As all its secrets are revealed?

The two of us will see the sky,
A clear and penetrating blue,
The morning sun will clarify
What you can trust, what will be true.

The day that passes in its course
Reveals the pattern of our lives,
Its light will show and re-enforce
The spring from which all else derives.

If we should see a cloud above
We will not let it mar the day,
For we will live within our love
And kiss the cloud away.

The sun will pass from east to west
From morning toward the night,
The day is slowly dispossessed
Of its reserve of light.

These journeys all run parallel
To our imperfect heart,
And when the sun has said farewell,
Will come a time to part.

Then come my love, and we will lie
Upon the summer grass,
And gaze into the endless sky
And watch the clouds that pass.

Perhaps the time will be fulfilling,
Our love intensify,
I cannot tell if you are willing,
But come and let us try.

MY FAIR YOUNG LADY

As my fair young lady goes
Within my life, unknowing,
She brings a light that always glows,
A beauty like a budding rose,
And leaves a sadness, going.

The early year had scarce begun
When first my virgin heart she stole;
She came in springtime with the sun
And, like the sun, she warmed my soul.

She stayed through summer and the fall;
The love I felt that we were sharing
Once seemed to satisfy, enthrall,
But finally could not forestall
My fear of loss, despairing.

The wind of winter, like a thief
Has from my life my lady taken,
The wind is not so sharp a grief
As candles by their flames forsaken.

But soon in spring a fresher green
Replaces leaves that fall and scatter,
And meanwhile snowfall, white and clean
Creates a world that is serene
Where sadness does not matter.

I know the cycle of the year
Will bring to bloom the cyclamen,
And dormant flowers will appear,
And long dead hopes will live again.

So I shall wait and wonder when
(With hope, like ashes, hardly burning),
I shall have my heart again
The day I know, and only then,
My lady is returning.

ADVICE

The young man came to me and said
He needed knowledge of
What in his life might lie ahead
And how to cope with love.

He was convinced beyond a doubt
That he was virtuous,
But did not wish to die without
Some time less tedious.

For innocence has many merits,
But rapture is not one,
Discretion that we might inherit
Is safe, but is not fun.

He wished to know what he should do
When love was imminent;
How could he know if it were true,
And not an accident?

Why he chose me for this instruction
I truly could not tell,
Remembering my introduction
To passion's carousel.

I summoned up the way I was
When I was just his age,
Imagining utopias
That I might soon engage.

For I myself had watched the whirl
Of gaudy forms and secret shapes,
And dreamed of some exciting girl
Through whom naivety escapes.

I rode the carousel around
Its endless arc for many years,
And sometimes thought that I had found
A love without the tears.

Whenever I imagined one
I ceased the senseless revelry,
That I perhaps had overdone
When I was fancy-free.

Abandoning the shallow roles
Which all of us affected,
I shunned the superficial goals
That careless girls expected.

I then became an earnest lover,
Respectable and grave,
Expecting that she would discover
How well I could behave.

But love was something I would find
That needed even more,
It often would, if misaligned
Be empty, as before.

Affection is reciprocal
And balanced equally,
When it is unilateral
It is illusory.

I had unlocked my virgin heart
When there was someone there,
I did not know she would depart
Before I was aware.

There is no place for selfishness
Or temporary vows,
Disloyalty will cause distress
That true love disallows.

I reconsidered his request,
And sadly I replied
That I myself had not been blessed,
No matter how I tried.

For I recalled my early love
To whom I had committed
Before I knew the outcome of
Affection counterfeited.

I could not be a hypocrite
And thus pretend it was not so,
I had to honestly admit
I truly did not know.

INVITATION TO THE DANCE

There was a time when we were young,
Indeed, our world was immature,
For all of those we lived among
Alike were confident and sure.

We all believed in our illusions
And thought that they would last forever,
As you today may have delusions,
And so repeat our blind endeavor.

Then innocence was universal,
As we assembled for a dance
That later proved to be rehearsal
For what our passion would enhance.

We saw each other at a distance
Across a large, disordered throng,
Attraction overcame resistance,
Anticipation was too strong.

As if to reach a secret pearl
A path is traced within a shell,
An involuting convex whorl,
For us, two curves in parallel.

We circled slowly through the crowd
In silence as they often parted
To clear a pathway which allowed
We two to meet, then music started.

The dance began without a touch
And with no certain expectation,
For neither knew what was too much
Excess of unforeseen elation.

The song continued, but we heard
A variation from the rest
Who listened, but who were not stirred
By feelings felt but not expressed.

And so we watched each other's eyes
To see the mutual emotion
Which once expressed, might then arise
Into a level of devotion.

I heard the rustle of your dress
As we came close to one another,
And by some magic could suppress
The nearby sound of any other.

Then coming even closer still
We touched, your hand laid into mine,
And with self-conscious lack of skill
Our bodies met, to intertwine.

Still insecure, we moved together,
Directed by the rhythmic pulse,
As winds will blow a floating feather,
Still unaware of its results.

I sensed a new aroma rising
Both powerful and prominent,
Beyond the scope of recognizing,
A fresh, unprecedented scent.

I knew it came from someone near
Who had not been so close before,
It stays with me, a souvenir
To mark the fragrance that you wore.

It truly represented you,
And went away when you were gone,
But even yet its residue
Is in my mind, and so lives on.

Emotions, which had first arisen
(But softly) when you caught my eye,
Had grown so strong that like a prison
They shrouded those who tried to fly.

Imprisoned by our own volition,
Encircled by the sight and sound,
We both were led into submission
By hidden feelings we had found.

So held together by the stirring
Excitement of someone so near,
Not told what we would be incurring,
We kissed, and crossed a new frontier.

A kiss allows one to explore
Those never-seen and secret spaces
With taste a thrill not felt before,
Unknown, unique, in hidden places.

Most intimate of all the senses,
A taste requires internal touch
And willingness, without defenses
That might distract delight too much.

The music adds its innuendo,
Suggesting passion with its pulse,
It rises into its crescendo,
Begetting unforeseen results.

Its climax came as we, together,
Were close as any two could be,
Encircled by a tight-wound tether
Of eagerness and ecstasy.

Then suddenly the dance was finished,
And we, exhausted from emotion
Encountered potency diminished,
And could not carry on our motion.

The music faded, then it ceased,
And all the crowd soon went away,
The rapture of the night decreased,
Revealing what it overlay.

Our passion proved illusionary,
And far too great would be its cost,
For pleasure was but momentary,
While prior innocence was lost.

The cruel paradox of life
Is that our need to seek, unite,
Is sharp and keen as any knife,
But blunts itself on morning's light.

For with the day, the music ceases,
The band itself is all dispersed,
Emotions, which are mere caprices
Have crested, and are now reversed.

And we return to an existence
Upon an ordinary plane,
The dance remembered at a distance
That we may never cross again.

Who knows what ecstasy is worth?
It passes swiftly, is no more,
Our lives are lived upon this earth,
And we are as we were before.

THE CHERRY TREES

The cherry trees in virgin white
Appear in early morning light,
As if they wish for all to see
This evidence of purity.

Immaculate in early spring
The trees a chaste appearance bring;
This modest fantasy will last
Until its season, brief, is past.

I lay with you upon the grass
And waited for the day to pass,
Anticipating that the night
Would bring some sensual delight.

The petals falling from the trees
Came dancing in the morning breeze,
And as we lay upon the ground
Descended on us, all around.

Then, waiting as each snowy petal
Might drift and float, and then would settle,
I asked, not certain what I meant
If you were, also, innocent.

As I remember, you replied:
"As virtuous as any bride,"
And so you were, and I was too,
For that was when our love was new.

The summer sunlight rearranged
The trees' appearance, and they changed
From flawless white that we had seen
To colors complex, mostly green.

Then what we never had expected,
The course of nature we neglected,
The cherries grew there, unforeseen,
And no one then could intervene.

Its branches bent by weight of fruit,
Each tree was bowed, a parachute,
But one which might or might not serve
To save one by its convex curve.

This transformation of a style
To one more like to last awhile
Could possibly have been predicted
And both our lives not been constricted.

The laws of nature never change,
They did, and do, and will arrange
Survival of an abstract life,
Regardless of our private strife.

Our individual distress
Or personal unhappiness
Means nothing in the master plan
That will ensure the life of Man.

The cherry's pure and bridal white
Will fade, for this will expedite
A course that cannot be completed,
A cycle endlessly repeated.

Soon autumn changes green to brown
And later, leaves will tumble down,
And then the winter's barren air
Will leave the branches stark and bare.

Our virtue, pure when we began
Would prove to last no longer than
The cherry's virginal display
Which all too soon would fall away.

III. REALITIES

"Return often and take me,
beloved sensation, return and take me
when the memory of the body awakens,
and old desire again runs through the blood;
when the lips and skin remember,
and the hands feel as if they touch again.
Return often and take me at night,
when the lips and the skin remember."

C.P. Cavafy

ADVENT

When I was younger, I did well alone,
And so did you, until a certain age
When life, while entering a complex stage
Revealed some features we had never known;
And that was when the two of us were thrown
As if by random fortune to engage
With one another, on a pilgrimage,
To seek and solve these questions on our own.
Confusion, our opponent, fell away,
And two became complete, as one was not.
A balanced pair produces symmetry,
And order which replaces disarray
Which fate determines that it should allot
To those insisting on autonomy.

REMNANTS

Come let me show you where to find
The scattered remnants of my heart
That once were welded, well aligned,
But since you left have flown apart.

Once we were young and life benign,
In love we both were amateurs,
But I was sure your heart was mine,
And certain that my own was yours.

For this is how, in early spring
Young lovers, filled with self-assurance
Enjoy their passion's wakening,
But give no thought to its endurance.

In summertime our love is tested
By endless days and fleeting nights,
In sunlight it is soon divested
Of flights of fancy and delights.

This bright illumination shows
Reality, straightforwardness,
That will by light of day expose
Our fantasies, now meaningless.

While twilight authorizes dreams
And darkest night conceals defects,
The clarity of day redeems
The plans of careless architects.

Our lives, predestined by some other
Designer, show that they are founded
On lasting linkage to another,
And on this rock true love is grounded.

Then time, which crushes all illusion,
Exposes dreams and reveries
As false and fanciful confusion,
And shows correct realities.

And through affliction we discover
What may be true, what temporary,
And whether our erotic lover
Will prove to be a sanctuary.

As summer stretches into fall,
Emotion at its best matures
From fleeting passions that enthrall
To constant caring that endures.

Among us, some will pass this test
And sense their souls' priorities,
Become a gracious host whose guest
Will always feel himself at ease.

Their essence and their heart intact
They face their lives with confidence,
No hazards, present or abstract
Can bring a threat of consequence.

But there are others, not so favored
Who absolutely had committed
Their lives to someone who then wavered,
Whose loyalty was counterfeited.

Someone whose lover has departed
Must find a new resilience,
In spite of being broken-hearted,
Restore their own self-confidence.

Then even when their faith is shattered
They grieve awhile, but when that ceases,
They summon once again the scattered,
Disordered but untarnished pieces.

With these attempts they clarify
And demonstrate their character,
Retrieve the remnants where they lie
To re-assemble as they were.

And this you mended perfectly;
Your heart, which shows no imperfections,
No trace of ambiguity,
Now faces redesigned directions.

I too encountered that endeavor,
I saw the fragments where they lay,
But I was neither strong nor clever,
And so the wind blew them away.

Thus I myself have not retrieved
Emotional self-confidence
That I could never be deceived,
And that has made the difference.

In winter, we feel much regret
For those we knew and then forgot,
Our memories will fade, and yet
Remember love as it was not.

THE ROVING HEART

Her heart, it went a-wandering
To places mine could never follow,
We carved our names into a tree
But found the tree was hollow.

The roving heart will come, will go,
But will not stay until tomorrow,
It brings a brilliant love, but oh,
It leaves eternal sorrow.

Her heart, it went a-wandering
Its fields of love were always fallow,
We tested depths of feeling, but
We found them to be shallow.

The roving heart will come, will go,
Its instrument a mournful cello
That alters springtime greens that glow,
To autumn shades of red and yellow.

Her heart, it went a-wandering
But always turning toward a mirror,
Where every love and every look
Would show her beauty clearer.

The roving heart will come, will go,
It will not earn but only borrow;
It builds accounts of grief and woe,
And pays with endless sorrow.

THE DRAGONFLY

In summertime the dragonfly
Will hover, humming, in the air
Between the earth and distant sky,
And will not settle anywhere.

And as it wavers, so its hue
Maintains an iridescent sheen,
A blend of shifting Prussian blue
And brilliant, hard metallic green.

It moves and darts into the wind,
Maneuvers quickly, so that each
Adjustment, wary, disciplined,
Can keep it there, just out of reach.

Then, after gazing with intent
But cautious eyes at all around,
As if surprised or diffident
It goes away, without a sound.

It shifts the angles of its wings
So slightly that they seem the same,
But then as if on puppet-strings
Is gone as swiftly as it came.

My love came close, but would not hold
The heart that I to her extended,
She said a love cannot grow old
If unengaged, and just pretended.

And so we circled, did not touch
In any close or loving way,
And any time I tried to clutch,
I felt her flinch and shy away.

She lingered, just as long as she
Felt independent, in control,
And while she felt security
She gave her presence, not her soul.

But dangers of commitment rose
And so she hovered, out of range;
When it was time to choose, she chose
Another shift, another change.

She held my hand, but lightly, so
The contact would not underscore
Affection she would soon outgrow;
We shared a space, but nothing more.

I wish her luck of every kind,
I hope her pleasures will not die,
And trust that she will never find
A lover like a dragonfly.

THE STALKING TIGER

The stalking tiger in the night
Can sense the prey for whom the sight
Alone may paralyze and will
Provide him with an easy kill.

Today we live on higher planes,
Politeness means that one abstains
From freely hunting one another,
No longer do we eat each other.

But still anxieties create
A constant need to dominate,
For who has true self-confidence
Without someone's subservience?

We lovers always interact
As if our love could re-enact
The best encounter of our lives,
The one through which our soul revives.

But there are some who, not so pure,
Are yet attractive, and will lure
Responses from the ones who need
Their ego to be guaranteed.

Then if you may be one of those
Whom God in His own wisdom chose
To be so credulous, you must
Beware to whom you give your trust.

Whenever you, in darkness dancing
Submit to one you find entrancing,
Imagine that your love conceals
The true imperatives he feels.

Not one of all of us presents
Ourselves in honest innocence,
And who can say in what disguise
Your lover looks into your eyes?

EXPERIENCE

When I was young and in my prime
My mentors told me that I should
Pursue a love with whom I would,
For someday there would come a time
When I no longer could.

At first, accepting their advice,
I roamed around from girl to girl,
I found some precious as a pearl,
Yet everyone I could entice
I drew into my whirl.

But soon these things I had believed
Became abruptly, overnight,
Much less a pleasure than a blight,
And then I knew I'd been deceived,
My mentors only halfway right.

It was my lack of constancy
That led the girls in unison
To seek a more devoted one;
The price of insincerity
Was to be left with none.

How could I quarrel with someone
Whose self-respect would not allow
Belief in some deceitful vow
Which would be credited by none
I might encounter now.

As I proceeded through the course
Of dissolute and brief relations,
I never saw the aberrations
Which mentors never would endorse,
But which were their creations.

Then I grew old, alone and tired,
For everyone had gone away;
I realized, to my dismay
My shallow season had expired,
My youth a runaway.

For each of all the girls I'd known
Declined to be a courtesan,
And chose a constant, faithful man;
Each found a love to call her own,
While I no longer can.

THE LOVERS

Some see two lovers on the street
Together in the afternoon,
And think, "Where will they later meet
To love each other, and how soon?"

I see the spaces in between
As signs that they will separate,
I wonder what is unforeseen,
That they do not anticipate.

The lovers walk, now hand-in-hand
And sometimes one will shyly clutch
An arm as if they understand
This prelude to a closer touch.

I see their hands part company
As each of them reclaims their own,
And though they keep a symmetry,
They move as two, now each alone.

Some will imagine how they meet
Again, together late at night,
And circumspect or indiscrete
They love by moon, or candle-light.

But I retain my own belief:
This fantasy is incomplete,
For passion all alone is brief,
And even love is bittersweet.

They sleep as close as two can sleep
Or sometimes even closer yet,
But time will pass, it will not keep,
The dawn will come and bring regret.

For waking, lovers find that they
Into reality emerge,
Beneath the urgent light of day
Their lives must for a while diverge.

They promise they will re-unite,
And many times indeed they can,
But subsequent to their delight
They find themselves where they began.

Despite the overwhelming urge
To form a single entity,
Two bodies cannot ever merge,
They keep their own identity.

And so their lives will alternate
Between the love that they will share
And solitude that will create
One person, but one-half a pair.

The irony of life is this:
In spite of love that they have known,
Someday will come a final kiss,
Then in the end they are alone.

IV. GOLDEN EARRINGS

"To certain people there comes a day
when they must say the great Yes or the great No.
He who has the Yes ready within him
reveals himself at once, and saying it he crosses over
to the path of honor and his own conviction.

He who refuses does not repent.
Should he be asked again he would
say No again. And yet
that No, the right No, crushes him
for the rest of his life."

C.P. Cavafy

THE BURNISHED FIRE

When golden earrings gleam within the night,
A burnished fire that often seems to dance
When touched by errant beams of candlelight,
They represent the promise of romance.
They are not only marks of elegance,
But symbols of pure magic at its height,
And gypsies know their golden radiance
Will bring two hearts together to unite.
The stories gypsies tell are often true,
And when they speak of seeing in the dark
A mystic image drawing one into
Its circle, they are thinking of this arc.
For golden earrings glow, forever new,
And if you wear them, love will come to you.

THE GYPSY CARAVAN

We danced by candlelight to violins
Outside a small café somewhere in France,
The melodies had gypsy origins
Suggesting magic, beauty and romance.

I still remember that the town's café
Was on one side of half a village square
And colored lanterns kept the night at bay,
Like sentinels that floated in midair.

Across the open square a caravan
Had come the night before and set their tents
So that the families within the clan
Had spaces equal to their prominence.

One tent was somewhat larger then the rest,
And occupied the center of the ring,
I later learned that this (as I had guessed),
Contained the household of the gypsy king.

They might be gone tomorrow, but tonight
They changed the square into a carnival,
Where vibrant lanterns shone with dancing light,
And music flowed, as if continual.

Musicians, clowns and jugglers all performed
To entertain (and profit from) the crowd,
Around the square the gypsy children swarmed,
As menacing as adults, if allowed.

A deft magician did a magic trick,
By making strangers' money disappear,
Returning it with gestures that were quick,
(If real or counterfeit was never clear).

The jewelry for sale was clearly cheap,
From gaudy necklaces to secret lockets,
The crowds, I thought, were herded past like sheep,
And so I guarded closely all my pockets.

The fortune-teller looked into your eyes
And saw the golden earrings you displayed,
Before she took your hand to analyze
The features that directed her charade.

"You will find love," she said, but did not say
If it were somewhere else or close at hand,
Nor whether it would last or fade away,
And, at that time, I did not understand.

But I have learned by hard experience
The truth that she had prior knowledge of:
Life has no certainty or permanence,
The golden earrings promise only love.

They do not indicate where it might lie,
Or who will be there at the magic time,
Or whether it will last and satisfy,
Or be a pretense, or a pantomime.

When morning came, the carnival was gone,
The square itself was vacant and forsaken,
For long before, the caravan moved on,
So no one realized what they had taken.

In our own lives together, their existence
Would mark the highest peak of our romance,
The gypsy violins lent their assistance,
Contributing the music for our dance.

The golden earrings that you wore could not
In latter days protect our fragile love,
But neither one of us could know just what
The rings and love itself consisted of.

For later, love that we had thought was true
Became like sand within an hourglass,
Alone, the gypsy fortune-teller knew
The thinly coated rings were made of brass.

THE PASSING OF TIME

Time is constant only for the chosen,
A certain Montague and Capulet,
Who paid a price to have their feelings frozen
Forever as they were when they first met.

Alone to these, and to the gods above
Will come no alteration, nor a change
In value or intensity of love,
All other passions time will rearrange.

We all begin our lives as innocent,
And layer lessons on as time goes by,
Complexity is not an accident,
But what we must accept and clarify.

And each of us must look within their heart
For secret places where one wind blows true,
So that two lovers never grow apart,
But at each shifting phase they will re-new.

For each must know that life may well demand
A change with time, becoming different
From that which we expected or had planned,
And early love is seldom permanent.

When we were young and time was infinite,
We looked ahead and saw a seamless flow
That swept us through our lives, an exquisite
Protracted, flourishing scenario.

But at some stage each one of us will learn
That life, like any drama, comes in acts
With intermissions, actors may return,
But find re-formed relations, altered facts.

In Buddhist monasteries, meditation
Occurs at intervals, all well defined,
By senior monks who warn the congregation
With bells and quiet chanting, intertwined.

The bell may ring so softly that a few
Could miss its signal, which I must admit
Includes myself but certainly not you,
Who knew when to, when not to re-commit.

You heard the bell while I was unaware,
Oblivious to changes in our love,
You found a new affection you could share,
Contentment that I still was dreaming of.

Two lie together, but their blood's a rover,
And passing time's a thing they cannot keep;
They must awaken, when the journey's over
There always will be time enough to sleep.

THE YEAR OF OUR LOVE

I used to believe, in the days I was pure,
(And I *was* pure, like you used to be),
That virtue and beauty combined were secure
And love would be stable for me.

I knew that your elegance, second to none
Would always command my affection,
And trusted the sharing that we had begun
Would never encounter rejection.

Attraction began, and continued to grow
From passion that flared in the night,
To constant devotion, a steady plateau
Of caring that still could excite.

It lasted that way through the year of our love,
And would have much longer if we
Had not been deluded by fantasies of
An effortless future to be.

Each seemed to be just what the other desired,
With qualities perfectly matched,
Since you were the beauty that all then desired,
And I came with honor attached.

For I was too innocent then to suspect
That others admired you as well,
The tales of flirtations were not incorrect,
(Those you were too cautious to tell).

Your loveliness was what would prove universal,
My trust was a limitless trait,
I could not believe that our love was rehearsal
For others that you might await.

Pure beauty is restless while seeking its equal,
While faith will stay firmly in place,
Our love was predestined to watch as its sequel
Approached at an unrestrained pace.

There always were others more handsome than I,
And all were attracted to you,
They were the excitement I could not supply,
The pleasures that you found anew.

I left for one minute, which did not seem long,
And found, on returning, the ending
Of what we had loved and had danced to, our song,
A conclusion beyond any mending.

And that was the moment that I realized
That passion might last for a day,
Or a month or a year if it was improvised
But true love would not go away.

Our timing was wrong, because I yet believed
In faithfulness, trust and devotion;
As you were enlightened, I still was deceived,
Maintaining my naïve emotion.

It took but an instant upon my return
To lose what I thought I possessed,
But most of a lifetime to find and discern
The values that truly were best.

And while I recovered from what I once had
And tried once again to discover
A love that was true and would never be sad,
I thought of you with your new lover.

I hope you were happy, for some time at least,
With passion that matched what we'd known;
This new love arising before ours had ceased
Was never completely your own.

Unless there is final, complete separation
From something you thought you outgrew,
The most genuine, new and impassioned relation
Inherits a veiled residue.

There is one reality that I am sure
Had never occurred to you two:
Emotion is seldom enough to secure
A love that survives and is true.

Two beautiful beings create an attraction
As strong as a magnet's two poles,
And who could resist such a potent reaction,
And who would consider controls?

Years later I heard that your new love was flawed,
Not perfect as you had believed,
The first time you looked in his eyes you were awed,
But soon enough, you were deceived.

However, by then it was late to repair
The internal faults that appeared;
Your beauty had foolishly been unaware
Of the distance his values had veered.

I learned from that episode never to trust
The loveliness I saw in you
Without a comparable sense that it must
When committed, be equally true.

For loyalty, faithfulness, upright behaviors
Are evident only through years
Of constant companionship, but are the saviors
Through times in which trouble appears.

Since the moment I saw you the very last time,
I have never encountered a love
With the glorious brilliance that then seemed sublime,
But instead sought a level above.

I changed my priorities toward the complete
And mature definition of living,
Which might be less blissful, perhaps bittersweet,
But certainly is more forgiving.

And having achieved a true love of my own,
I freely look back on our past;
I hope you remember the love we had known
And its memory always will last.

THE STRENGTHENING OF ELEMENTS

The elements parade across the page,
Maintaining intervals as they are able,
Each one alone, unique upon its stage,
Its square within the periodic table.

Beginning first with hydrogen, then helium,
Pursued by antimony, arsenic,
Advancing to aluminum, selenium,
And countless others, many pages thick.

Some elements, in general opaque,
Conduct electric currents, storing heat,
And some of these, called *metals,* may partake
Of useful functions in the world they meet.

A metal may be pure, or some composite
Of elements combined by means of fusion,
A process so complete that no deposit
Or residue remains at its conclusion.

The basest metals, such as iron or lead,
(That oxidize or easily corrode),
Exist alone, but are not coveted
Because of weaknesses that each one showed.

Pure iron will rust, is relatively weak,
The softer lead corrodes in air, indents,
But both may gain the properties we seek
By fusion with some other elements.

Thus iron plus carbon equals stainless steel
(With chromium and nickel in the mix),
And lead with tin and copper is ideal
To form the pewter used in candlesticks.

The nobler compounds, such as brass or bronze
Are made of copper, fused with zinc or tin,
And constitute the bells of carillons
And common objects, like a safety pin.

There are some noble metals which are rare,
Including silver, platinum and gold;
Although they are called *precious*, they must share
A blend, or be too soft to shape or mold.

A precious metal often is defined
By scarcity and value (which is high),
Especially when purity combined
With brilliance and with luster catch the eye.

But even precious metals must be fused
With certain other lower elements,
They must be hardened, stiffened to be used,
With tensile strength to give resilience.

To make a silver *Sterling*, one must add
Some copper in a pre-determined measure,
To purest gold there are a myriad
Of additives to this expensive treasure.

Among the elements considered proper
To give pure gold its necessary denseness
Are nickel and palladium and copper,
And silver to increase its light's intenseness.

Our early loves are like these elements,
Arising in a simple perfect state,
Until confronted by the evidence
Of loss that we could not anticipate.

And then the trust, that had been infinite
Is modified by our experience,
Becoming more selective, we commit
With lesser passion, but more permanence.

Our lives begin like bullion bars of gold,
As pure as possible, but simply shaped,
Whose vast potential, stirring to behold,
Remains concealed until it has escaped.

As gold is *tempered*, gaining strength for rings,
And fused with other elements, *alloyed*,
So life must undergo, throughout its length
Events that we endeavor to avoid.

73

The disappointments and the loss of love
To which we are repeatedly exposed
Transform naïveté in favor of
A knowledge of ourselves once undisclosed.

The gypsies know illusions cannot last;
The rest of us believe, at least at first,
Before our age of innocence is past,
That life and love need never be rehearsed.

But all of us will learn, and be much wiser
As hard experience creates maturity;
If passion goes away, the equalizer
Is newly found devotion, and security.

Like purest precious metals, we are soft
Until subjected to a crucible,
In which a fire will raise our lives aloft
And lift them to their very pinnacle.

REGRET

If I believed we could return
And be once more the way we were,
I would endeavor to discern
And sharpen feelings now a blur.

I can recall initial bliss,
But cannot quite remember why
It seemed compelling, nor why this
Of all your loves would fade and die.

When we were young, we both pretended
That we were meant for one another
And no one else, and so, depended
On not desiring any other.

But those who love, when love is new
Can never know if it will last,
Exciting and inspiring, true,
Until its promises are past.

Assurances of faithfulness
When broken, cannot be repaired,
Regrets that someone may express
Can never prove they truly cared.

A fragile love, like crystal, shatters
Into a thousand brilliant pieces,
No effort to repair it matters,
And soon our senseless striving ceases.

We sadly sweep the scattered glass,
And fragments of the memories
That still may touch us as we pass
Into new loves or fantasies.

For always, there will be regrets
For might-have-beens that never were,
Enduring love that hope begets,
Potential that is now a blur.

The images that we believe,
And take each night into our dreams
Prove only that what we conceive
Is never truly what it seems.

V. THE LOVERS

"Along the field as we came by
A year ago, my love and I,
The aspen over stile and stone
Was talking to itself alone.
'Oh who are these that kiss and pass?
A country lover and his lass;
Two lovers looking to be wed,
And time shall put them both to bed'........

......While overhead the aspen heaves
Its rainy-sounding silver leaves
And I spell nothing in their stir;
But now perhaps they speak to her
And plain for her to understand
They talk about a time at hand
When I shall sleep with clover clad,
And she beside another lad."

A.E. Houseman

BRIEF ENCOUNTER

We came together, since our roads ran near,
So close that we could speak, and pausing there,
I found a sudden lightness in the air.
Lonely past times seemed to disappear
And through your eyes the world was new and clear;
But since ahead of you were places where
I could not go, and things I could not share,
You held me close, just once, and left me here.
Now I will stay a while and watch you go,
Glad because the thoughts of you I hold
Will warm my life and light a world grown old,
But always with a sadness for I know
The love I never found in any part
Of all the world is there within your heart.

I REMEMBER

My love was like no other girl
That I had ever known,
Her hair was long, a golden swirl
And at her throat a single pearl
Was always there, alone.

Some other eyes that I had seen
Were gray, or brown, or brilliant green,
But her's were of a different hue,
A deep and clear and cobalt-blue.

She never moved without a grace
That all who saw her noted,
While others through an equal space
Might glide or drift from place to place,
It always seemed she floated.

Her face was bright as morning sun,
The very essence of "esprit",
I never knew another one
Who turned a smile like that to me.

Yet, far beyond the look she sent
Into my waiting eyes,
I was not sure to what extent
She was sincere, or what she meant,
But I could fantasize.

And so I did, and all the while
That I was willingly deceived,
So many others shared her smile
That which of you would have believed?

So now I wander through the world
Where somewhere she has flown,
And wonder whether she has whirled
From love to love, or has she curled
Into herself alone?

And if we should, by accident
Meet somewhere, once again,
Would there be some acknowledgement
Of what had happened then?

Or is it likely she forgot
The things that did not last,
Would she remember me, somewhat,
Or was I just a hidden dot
Within a checkered past?

No matter, I will still recall
Her beauty, crystalline,
The way she smiled at me, and all
That I had thought we'd been.

THE MORNING AND THE EVENING STAR

Our love when we first met was like
The morning and the evening star,
Delight and dawn are as alike
As peace and twilight are.

Unequalled was the evening star
That we once watched on summer nights,
Its presence there was singular,
A priest with acolytes.

It settled in the western sky
As daylight slowly disappeared,
The spreading dusk would magnify
The light that persevered.

It traced the pathway of the sun
But stayed an interval behind,
So when the night had well begun
The sky was re-defined.

It followed close behind the moon
With both descending two-abreast,
And far beyond, the sky was strewn
With tiny stars, recessed.

The others flickered, glittering,
But ours was constant, warm,
And with extensions on each wing
Seemed almost cruciform.

It caught our eyes, and dominating
The early, fading western sky,
It hung above the moon, awaiting
A love to certify.

The morning and the evening star
Are both the same, they are a planet,
Mysterious and similar
To love, when we began it.

We gazed upon the morning star
That seemed at first so permanent,
But faded with the day ajar,
And who knew where it went?

The morning star retains its glow
While light of dawn is coming near,
Until the sun begins to grow,
And then will disappear.

We saw the evening star at night
And made those vows we swore to keep
As lovers swear by candle light,
And then we fell asleep.

Our love was like the morning star
Still shining when we woke at dawn,
It seemed at first spectacular
But soon enough was gone.

The morning and the evening stars,
Intense as any light can be
Comprise the total repertoires
Of lovers, such as we.

For love is magical at night
When faith depends upon illusion,
But when the sun brings out its light
It clarifies confusion.

For then the stars must go away,
The planets, too, reluctantly,
Our loves, if foreordained to stay
Must face reality.

Our lives go on throughout the day
But not idyllic as at night,
Their well-lit course will wear away
The vows of candlelight.

And yet, still some of us endure
Throughout this ordinary time;
Uncertain, often insecure,
Our love may prove sublime.

If we observe and meditate,
The morning and the evening star
Each in its way will illustrate
What we together are.

CANDLES

We lit a candle, you and I,
And vowed our love would never end,
Whatever painful might pass by,
Our lives, united, would transcend.

The future held no fear for us
For early love was incandescent,
And that which seemed so virtuous
Would prove eternal and incessant.

We thought our universe was static
And we ourselves would never change,
Emotions would remain ecstatic
With nothing we need re-arrange.

But we forgot that love and light
Cost more than anyone assumed,
While burning brightly through the night
The candle is itself consumed.

When passion dies, then love will follow
Unless the lovers can rebuild,
The used receptacle stays hollow
Until it once again is filled.

Untended candles gutter down
Creating flumes of melted wax,
Until the flame itself will drown
Submersed in rising cul-de-sacs.

A love must always grow or die,
Develop depth or blow away
With any wind, it must defy
The lures that lead to disarray.

A light must be re-lit before
It grows so dim one cannot see,
The flickering that we ignore
Becomes pure darkness, suddenly.

To keep a total love alive
We must have faith and understand:
Those who would have their light survive
Keep many candles close at hand.

RECOVERY

There was a time when I was pure,
There was a time when you were too,
But both of us were immature
And neither knew a way to cure
Resentment as it grew.

And then a line that we both crossed
Condemned us to our present fate,
We could not comprehend the cost
Nor calculate what we had lost
Until it was too late.

I have not yet regained the trust
That I allowed to go astray,
My self-respect could not adjust
To feelings fleeting as the dust
That dries and blows away.

And are you also solitary,
Or have you found a newer lover?
Is he a stable sanctuary,
Or fantasy, or temporary,
So that we might recover?

If so, since we were equal then,
And equally we did allow
Erosion of a genuine
Affection, let us once again
Be true, beginning now.

THE HONEST MAN

To be at times an honest man
Is not so great a talent,
For I was one when we began
And I was young and gallant.

One's youth and charm hide many sins
But neither one will last,
And later, recompense begins
When both of these have passed.

Since I could answer honestly
Whatever you might ask,
I never thought sincerity
To be a daunting task.

But so it proved, and soon I found
To mine and your distress,
That instabilities surround
A lack of truthfulness.

To be a mostly honest man
Is difficult at best,
But I have done the best I can,
And left to God the rest.

If you should wish that I would say
That I will love you still
Forever, as I do today
Then I will say I will.

But love is something I have found
So many times before,
It always seems to come around
To die outside my door.

The door that I had opened once
But would not open twice
Became a rampart that confronts
The path to paradise.

To always be an honest man
Was quite beyond my reach,
It seemed to me utopian
And something I would breach.

You wished to know if I could love
With all my heart and soul,
But there were demons from above
Which I could not control.

Then these came down, encircled me,
And whispered in my car
Of fickle charms of vanity
I never wished to hear.

You asked if I would love forever,
But you misunderstood,
For I was neither wise nor clever,
And so I said I would.

To be a constant gentleman
Is what I should achieve,
But this is vastly harder than
You ever could conceive.

A gentleman provokes no pain
(Except by his intention),
For with restraint he will abstain
From causing apprehension.

The key is always to be kind
(Which I at times forgot),
This brings both peace and grace combined,
Some can, but I could not.

So you may ask, when I depart
If pathways I may choose
Might break a lover's fragile heart,
But never ask me whose.

FAITH

When I was young and so were you,
And all the world around was new,
We promised God we would be true
Forever, to each other.

But then we found as time went past
We shared a love that could not last
The heart that had been so steadfast
Was given to another.

Then as events and life went by
And time itself, which seemed to fly,
Recurrent dreams now verify
That memories remained.

And now we meet and wonder how
That we forgot that early vow,
A love that sadly passed, and now
Can never be reclaimed.

Remember well, when you are young
That all the songs you never sung
Like silent bells that have not rung
Are still throughout the night.

So hold the love that you have now
As long as time and fate allow,
And keep forever any vow
To faithfully unite.

VI. MEMORIES

"I should like to relate this memory,
but it is so faded now----scarcely anything is left----
because it lies far off, in the years of my early manhood.
A skin as if made of jasmine,
that night in August----was it August? That night,
I can just barely remember her eyes; they were, I think,
blue----ah yes, blue, a sapphire blue.

C.P. Cavafy

BUTTERFLIES

The moment that we felt our lives emerge
From their cocoons of youth and innocence,
We knew that life, now in its present tense
Was not complete, but somehow on its verge;
We underwent the universal urge
To seek each other, share experience
So life had purpose, not coincidence,
And all its varied pathways would converge.
We spread our wings up to the sky and sun,
And while they stretched and dried we hesitated
To ascertain that we were not alone;
Then only when we found in unison
The harmony we sought, no longer waited
But flew away together, on our own.

REUNION

We gathered after many years and wondered
What fragments of our former lives lived on
Beyond the past; the many times we blundered,
Had they been buried in oblivion?

In contrast, yes, there was much happiness,
Which seldom lasted longer than a year,
So transient that it seemed meaningless,
And if remembered, fleeting and austere.

But still, there may be one (not often two)
Significant encounter waiting there,
A debt unpaid, and now long overdue,
A once-intense, still unresolved affair.

And so I wandered through the careless crowd
To seek the resolution that I needed,
Prepared to meet someone who disavowed
Acknowledgment, or let it pass, unheeded.

And then I met someone I thought I knew,
Perhaps remembered from a former season,
When passion left its ruined residue
To reconstruct itself by using reason.

Unsettled, I began reluctantly,
No longer confident as I had been,
And almost frightened by uncertainty,
Was hesitant approaching you again.

But thoughts can easily outrun our words
That must be screened, examined, judged correct;
Arriving, vanishing like hummingbirds,
They bypass filters of our intellect.

"Are you the one I loved when we were young,
And if you are, do you remember me?
Have later lovers you have lived among
Erased my image in your memory?"

"I still remember when we met, for you
Were suddenly unique within the throng,
The multitude that I had wandered through
As if I had been searching all along."

"There were so many there, and all alike
Except for certain minor qualities
With which I fell in love, or might dislike,
Depending on my prejudice toward these."

"My interactions then were never deep,
Impressions seldom passed beyond initial,
But summoned fragile dreams that would not keep;
The beauty that I sought was superficial."

"Commitment then was casual and brief,
And that was just as well, my innocence
Encouraged fantasies that led to grief
When fascination turned to negligence."

"And each of us was like a cameo,
Two shadow-figures in the multitude,
Unformed and nebulous, who could not know
That our affair would be an interlude."

"Is yours the face I almost recognize,
Remembering the way it used to be?
Unfeeling age has added its disguise,
As I am certain it has altered me."

"The image I preserved in memory,
Your features as they were when you were young,
May well have been a dream, a fantasy,
But were a magic charm to which I'd clung."

"And as I seek the outlines of your face,
The symmetry, the facets that I knew,
I recognize what time cannot displace
But only add its surface marks onto."

"Façades will change in time, but what remains,
The essence of original appearances
May still be found beneath the rough terrains
That life produces, age's interferences."

"If it is true that eyes reveal the soul,
The deepest core, that otherwise lies buried,
Your eyes today would surely play that role,
And testify that yours has never varied."

You saw me at a distance, and you smiled,
But was that evidence of recognition,
Of ancient feelings, still unreconciled,
Or merely your yet gracious disposition?

Your smile and mouth, beyond analysis,
Evoke a memory suppressed for years,
In which within the moment of a kiss
A sense of isolation disappears.

It summoned up the time, so long ago
When you first turned your face to me and let
Intensities of feeling overflow
Into an image I remember yet.

I touched your mouth with mine, then gently traced
Its shape, extent, and modest separation,
And tasted flavors there that interlaced
With mine, and promised future consummation.

But that was just a dream, and what we felt
Was momentary, it could never last,
For in our innocence and youth we dwelt
In present time, not future or the past.

"Is yours the body that I lay beside
On summer afternoons when all was new?
While feelings, which remained ungratified,
Confused affection that I had for you."

"At first, we both were confident and sure,
But then became aware that life has rules
And consequences; we were insecure,
And with that limitation, passion cools."

"So while my fancy traced your curvature,
Imagining how pleasant it would feel,
I knew the consequence we would endure,
Commitment we no longer could conceal."

"Unable to provide what you deserved,
I reached a limit I could not extend;
But I remember contours, soft and curved,
And long smooth lines that never seemed to end."

"So when I said my personal good-byes
To all I knew with you, and to your face,
Your personality, your endless eyes,
I felt that I had lost my breathing-space."

"But that is what I did and what I lost,
And what I came to find a closure to,
An absolution from the moral cost
To which I introduced myself, and you."

"I had resolved to ask for an account
Of how you had reacted to the spell
Which passion had imposed, and what amount
Of sentiment you felt at our farewell."

"While reminiscing on our time together,
Perhaps you have re-written (I have not),
Our history, I often wonder whether
I learned from you much more than I forgot."

"Since first we met, and I was tentative,
Have you both found and kept a better man,
Who knew, maturely, how to love and give,
And does he still complete what I began?"

But when I saw you as you are today,
I knew that you had never felt regret
At love that we had known, that went away,
An apparition that you could forget.

So then I put away my fantasies,
Illusions I had kept for many years,
Once comforting, now proven false, and these
Were stored within a life-span's souvenirs.

And I was sure that you were not regretting
The memories and dreams of yesterday,
Not knowing these, or long-ago forgetting,
You smiled and said farewell, and went away.

And so did I, now free of self-deceit,
Which had invaded and remained a part
Of all my life, until this bittersweet
Event exposed it and released my heart.

A CLEAR AND CERTAIN PLACE

There once were warm and cordial places,
Congenial sanctuaries where
I always saw familiar faces
And we were welcome there.

The many lives in parallel
Among which we were two,
Revolved as on a carousel
From which no one withdrew.

Within that space we were secure
And no one thought to question whether
Our promises were premature,
Or would we stay together.

Indeed, the time seemed infinite,
And nothing ever could transform
Our self-assurance, nor admit
To an impending storm.

But things are seldom as they seem,
So often lovers are surprised
To find fidelity a dream,
Duplicity disguised.

The crowd, the circle, stayed the same
But patterns somehow re-arranged,
And like a silly, youthful game,
Assorted partners changed.

As if a signal, known to some
Was given in a secret way,
To banish equilibrium
And create disarray.

And disarray it did create
In hearts from whom a love had flown,
Some found another candidate,
And some were left alone.

But soon enough most closed the span
With many partners re-united,
And once again the dance began,
But I was not invited.

There is a refuge I once knew
Where I could go, but that was when
We were a pair, and both were true;
It will not come again.

With journeys finished, time is done,
The evening calls "Lie down and rest",
I will, and dream of us as one,
And that will be the best.

TRANSITION

Not long ago, we both were true
And faithful only to each other,
You were to me, and I to you,
With neither thinking of another.

But we were young, and youth is brief,
Pure passion could not last forever,
The years would pass, and like a thief
Maturity reshapes endeavor.

Those were the times when we could dream
Of lives that might approach perfection,
If there were faults, they were redeemed
And balanced by a love's protection.

Then grief had no reality,
And cares the lightness of a feather,
For life had no finality
When both of us were young together.

And when our love did not survive
The pain was sharp but it was brief,
Our future still remained alive,
Our next affair would bring relief.

A paradise may well exist,
And if it does we have been there,
If there was happiness we missed,
We knew that there was more to spare.

That season held what we expected,
The best of all fate would allow,
A golden pleasure-dome erected
When we were young; we are not now.

Our youth and beauty were a pair
Of fragile gifts beyond belief,
For jealous time (which will not share),
Makes certain that their term is brief.

When love begins in adolescence,
Intensity is unsurpassed,
With energy like incandescence
That is so bright it cannot last.

The years of youth are like a candle
That burns so eagerly at first,
But then is treacherous to handle
When in its own hot wax immersed.

The candle is extinguished, drowned,
A victim of consuming fire,
And early love is often found
Exhausted by its own desire.

If any virtue comes with age
It must be wisdom and restraint,
With no illusions we engage
What comes our way with no complaint.

But still I look into the past
At fantasies of how we were,
And dream of things that did not last
And yet I am their prisoner.

The greatest gift of older age
Is to recall without regret
The pleasures of a younger stage,
And memories that they beget.

If we would manage aging well
We would dismiss those early years,
And short-lived love, a sentinel
That only leaves us souvenirs.

Dismissing from our inner lives
Whatever thoughts are frivolous,
We should make sure that what survives
Will be sincere and serious.

And faith should supersede a passion
Which burns intensely, but consumes
Itself and is reduced to ashen
Memories in empty rooms.

Far better to have found the trust,
The confidence and inner peace,
Which will allow a love which must
Be resolute and never cease.

Now, many years past our affair,
We two have found two finer loves,
Where happiness is like two pair
Of pleasant, warm, well-fitted gloves.

DREAMS

He dreams, as old men often dream
Of days and loves long past,
And though at times they still can seem
As bright as any candle's gleam
Through years they cannot last.

"Do I remember my first love?
How foolish just to ask,
She shapes my dreams as would a glove
And lives within my heart, above
My antiquated mask."

"Pretending not to care protects
My inner self from shame
For memory itself affects
The image that each one selects
To show what he became."

"How could I ever once forget
Her presence, clear and bright,
Her aura, like a statuette,
But then beneath the coverlet
So warm throughout the night."

"But certainly I can recall
Each detail of her face,
The greater features and the small
The harmony which all-in-all
Was never commonplace."

"The years may lead the mind astray,
But this I know is true,
(As clearly as if yesterday):
Her eyes were brilliant green, or gray,
No, surely azure blue."

"How could I ever fail to see
The love I had when I
Was young and innocent and free,
She lives within my memory
And will until I die."

THE ROSE AWAKENS

A rose may stir in early spring,
Uncertain whether winter's cold
Will soon return, and lingering,
Inhibit its awakening,
And what will it withhold?

Inert and dormant through the freeze,
Yet living, deep within its center,
It may well wonder (with unease)
If summer's promised warming breeze
Is something it might enter.

The summons of the spring will come,
But may not be as evident
As one might wish, a pendulum
Without an equilibrium
And nothing permanent.

Awakened from inactive sleep
A love begins in much this fashion,
From far inside, at levels deep
And hidden, it will try to leap
Into an open passion.

A child's emotion, like the winter,
Is frozen by dictated order,
Repressed within its epicenter
So that no eagerness may enter,
Within an austere border.

Then suddenly, as with a wind,
Emotion senses its potential;
No longer strictly disciplined,
Unsure how far it might ascend,
It knows it is essential.

But still to be determined are
Parameters, and how they fit
Into a total life; how far
Will love be like a falling star?
What form will fate permit?

The rose, awake, is also sure
To grow with grace and symmetry,
But whether this will long endure
Or if its essence will be pure
Is lost in secrecy.

For it, aroused by warmth and light
Is captive to capriciousness,
Depending on a constant, bright
And reassuring sun that might
At times be valueless.

For mist and fog may interpose
Their darker, detrimental screen,
This interference will expose
The weakness of the growing rose
That no one had foreseen.

Whatever alters constant sun
Will cause a rose to grow deformed,
Without the beauty once begun,
Diminished by comparison
With it, if it were warmed.

Emotions, likewise sensitive
To affirmations of their worth,
Require respect for them to live,
Approval which someone may give,
That validates their birth.

The first opinion is our own,
We are the only ones who know
When youth and carelessness have shown
Their faithless side, and now full-grown,
Some things we must forego.

Now many pathways lead ahead,
In sunlight we can see them surely,
But we must choose which one, instead
Of being guided (or misled)
By others, immaturely.

What we affirm (or we refuse)
Determines our selected path,
It leads to lives that we would choose
Instead of those in which we lose,
And rue their aftermath.

The course of true fidelity,
The one we know that we should take,
Will not at first appear to be
The most exciting we can see,
Appearing a mistake.

But even those who, virtuous,
Are keen to trust when they begin,
Can follow faith as impetus
And pledge an honest effort plus
Devotion, may not win.

For, like the rose whose elegance
Is animated by the warm
Anticipated circumstance
(Which may be just a fleeting glance),
They still could come to harm.

The rose appearing near perfection
When favored by the early sun,
May still endure a new direction
If it is altered by rejection
Before it has begun.

The blighted rose was not to blame,
The fickle sunlight took its toll,
It governed what the flower became,
With flaws that roses can reclaim,
And once again be whole.

A love expressed but then betrayed
Must not be left to atrophy,
If it returns as mere charade
Or even worse, an escapade,
It will be judged unworthy.

Its perfect model is the rose,
Where grace reveals a new endeavor,
Its self-assurance will expose
A beauty that will never close,
And which will last forever.

VII. THE LOVER'S RESOLVE

"Today I shall be strong
No more shall yield to wrong,
Shall squander life no more;
Days lost, I know not how,
I shall retrieve them now;
Now I shall keep the vow
I never kept before.

A.E. Houseman

ALTERNATIVES

With sudden force, the mist around us clears,
We see our choices plainly, and we lose
The vague and careless life which we abuse,
The challenge of a different path appears.
We have within us, in our strengths and fears
The power to affirm or to refuse;
Pathways that we choose or do not choose
Determine now the course of future years.
Once denied, our open spaces close
And we have limited our future, never
Escaping from the patterns of the past;
But if accepted, we are like a rose,
Unfolding into beauty that forever
Surrounds us like a love that holds us fast.

PROMISES

To have a constant faithful lover
Is what we all should most desire,
But some of us may well discover
That passion often is a liar.

For love will promise many things
And some of them may yet come true,
But those who dream of wedding rings
May wait and find them overdue.

Infatuation often leads
To promises that are not kept,
Illusion frequently exceeds
The truth we must at last accept.

Beware, my love, believing me
And what I vow in times of passion,
True pledges of fidelity
Are not created in this fashion.

Commitment flourishes through time
Remaining true throughout the day,
While what so briefly seemed sublime
Within a minute drains away.

The foolish offer covenants
They know that they will never keep,
They do not see the relevance
That what they sow they later reap.

The wise will wait until the end
Of passion's silly fantasy,
And then will seek to comprehend
Its senseless ambiguity.

I will not be a hypocrite,
Denying what I have begot,
Not every person can commit,
Some can, and some cannot.

So come my love and let us share
Our pure sensation and emotion,
But do not ask that I declare
Eternal, infinite devotion.

And do not ask for promises;
Although I will not seek to stray,
I am not perfect, no one is,
So take the love I have today.

A pearl, no sudden accident,
Is built in layers over years
To ease unbearable torment
Equivalent to human tears.

So over time there will occur
Ill-fortune and the misery
That tests our basic character,
The limits of fidelity.

And it is then that we will find
What has evolved throughout our lives,
How essences are re-aligned,
And whether love like ours survives.

Then, if the fates or gods are kind,
And all goes well with us as one,
We may be equally inclined
To lengthen what we have begun.

And when the two of us can see
That our distinctive lives will fit
Into a single entity,
Then we together will commit.

THE ROSE

In spring the flowers on the hill
Salute the sun, arising,
Their color will come out until
The spectrum is surprising.

The crocuses are mainly white
But may be violet,
And growing closely may unite,
A visual duet.

The simplest yellow daffodils,
Are pure, like violins,
A darker hyacinth distils
The paints of porcelains.

The tulips are the most diverse,
Their colors gathering
The spectrum of the universe,
Yet do not live past spring.

Early, in his adolescence,
A young man looks for love,
As flowers search for iridescence
And seek the sun above.

But later, when the days are longer
And light is commonplace,
The hillside color grows much stronger,
And gains a special grace.

A rose grows slower than the rest,
Unfolding, one-by-one,
And seen alone, they are the best,
Beyond comparison.

The summer of our lives, a season
Of more maturity,
Gives us a chance (and greater reason)
To choose simplicity.

If we are wise, then like the rose
We will develop slowly,
Seek beauty similar to those
Whose innocence is holy.

And when we find an unclaimed heart
As virtuous as this,
We should reject its counterpart,
A short-lived artifice.

Though many flowers, seeming pure,
Are spread across the hill,
A wise man, one that is mature,
Rejects the daffodil.

A daffodil will live a day,
A week if it is stronger,
And we, when it has gone away,
Remember it no longer.

For it, and others of its kind
Rely on mass effects,
Ten thousand yellows, when combined
Disguise each one's defects.

To gather flowers that are wild
Brings transient delight
And satisfaction to a child
That will not last the night.

A man who takes a longer view
Renounces passing pleasure,
He chooses one whose faults are few,
A more abiding treasure.

He waits and picks one perfect rose
And keeps within his soul
The memory of what he chose
And what will make him whole.

For soon a thousand fleeting buds
Will open, bloom and die;
In autumn, melancholy floods
The life that passes by.

But he who holds within his being
A solitary essence
Of truth and virtue will be freeing
His spirit from senescence.

For soon the winter comes upon us,
The snow will cover hills,
Infirmity and age lie on us,
And countless are our ills.

And yet the memory sustains
And will alone suffice;
The beauty of the rose contains
The key to paradise.

And therefore, I remember you
As you were when we met,
At least the image will be true,
For I will not forget.

Some memories are fleeting things
This is not one of those,
No matter what our future brings
You will remain my rose.

But stems containing many thorns
Cause pain if held too tightly,
This inconvenient armor warns
To let the rose lie lightly.

When young, I could not disengage,
But held you closer yet,
And paid with pain, that now with age
I constantly regret.

If I had only been more wary,
And shared with all my heart
One flower so extraordinary,
We would not be apart.

COME LET US TRY

Come, let us try again to be
As we have been before,
For time has almost passed us by
And one full night before I die
I need to love once more.

For I was strong and handsome then
And you were light and fair,
And all who knew us knew that when
Which-ever needed hope again,
The other would be there.

They could not see into my soul
Or know my secret fears,
The weakness that would play its role
And over time would take its toll,
Creating endless tears.

The fault was mine, the anguish yours,
And had I ever known
The grief inconstancy assures,
The demons that this state conjures,
I would not be alone.

But I myself was mystified
That I, confused, had done
These things I would prefer to hide,
But those that could not be denied
Had only just begun.

For once consumed by foolishness
I felt somehow compelled
At very least to acquiesce
And took my folly to excess
An urge unparalleled.

So I maintained all through the years
A superficial course,
That had no center or frontiers
No ending, but which reappears
And seems to have no source.

All this is well while immature,
But all of its appeal
Relates to those who, insecure
Need constantly to reassure
A juvenile ideal.

Behavior is related to
The strength within a soul;
So I began my life anew,
Discarding folly I outgrew
And learning self-control.

I pray that it is not too late
For faith to be once more
Between us and to animate
A love that we may consecrate
As we had done before.

Then come, my love, and let us see
If fate is kind to us,
And if amid fidelity,
Restored enshrouded feelings, we
Emerge victorious.

THE HARVEST MOON

Our love was once the harvest moon,
Blood-orange in the eastern sky,
Complete and round when low, but soon
En route to smaller discs, when high.

Septembers at the equinox
Produce this strange phenomenon,
For once a year this paradox
Occurs, and then in days is gone.

And though the present, filled with passion
Arises through the azure blue
Of early evening, soon an ashen
Complexion gains a paler hue.

Requiring only several days,
A shadow eats into the ring;
No longer in its perfect phase
The circle shrinks, becomes a spring.

The moon eclipsed retains its essence,
Reality is not in doubt,
And though it loses incandescence,
Its light will once again come out.

A love imagined as a pure
And flawless symbol in the sky,
May find its once intact contour
Reduced or shattered, or awry.

Its colors, ardent and intense
May reach the limits of its ration,
With time may fade to reticence
And lose the vividness of passion.

Some mourn for things they never had,
Or briefly have and cannot keep,
Far better to rejoice, be glad
For harvest moons, both full and deep.

Their elegance among the stars
And planets of celestial space
Comes once a year, for some this mars
Perfection passing times erase.

But I am grateful to have known
Within my life one flawless time,
And if it seemed to be on loan
It still was, for a while, sublime.

And even should a shadow steal
Across the sky to separate
Reality from an ideal
Illusion which we might create,

We cannot lose the memory
Regardless of how long we live,
This interlude will always be
 Our ultimate affirmative.

For you and I together shared
A lovely sight, a synthesis
Of line and color, fully paired,
As pure and perfect as our kiss.

VIII. THE EVOLUTION OF LOVE

"I have prayed, O memory,
to find in you the best guide, that I might
make the face of one I loved as it once used to be....

I have created our love in joy and in sorrows,
out of so many circumstances, out of so many things.
You have become all feeling for me."

C.P. Cavafy

THE GROWTH OF DEVOTION

I'd celebrate your grace, say you were fair,
For so you are, but this is not so much
To sing about, a thousand might compare
In part to you, and yet I would not touch
Their names with praise. And would I love you then
The less if you were plain? I will not say
That beauty is your only essence when
I'd love you still, if you were not that way.
I'd rather honor virtue, in the sense
Of constant caring for me, this alone
Sets you apart. Among the past events
And people, through the years that I have known,
There is one thing that only we can share,
A time I needed you, and you were there.

DISCOVERY

I found you in the morning, where
The grass was bright with dew;
Your smile and laugh were light as air,
Your face and form were wondrous fair,
And all the world was new.

The hills were light by highest sun,
The fields were bright between,
Your flawless face appeared as one
Surpassed in beauty there by none,
The fairest ever seen.

The shadows steal the sight away,
And now remains the sound,
Your gentle voice that does convey
Comfort to the passing day,
And peace to all around.

I feel you with me through the night
Your spirit holds me fast,
And guides me as a candle's light
That gives my soul a second sight
Until the dark is past.

Though swiftly fades the night, my love
So that we soon may see
The sun dissolve the stars above
Still you shall be my light, my love,
Through all the days to be.

COVENTRY

Once people came to Coventry
To search for meaning in their lives,
To sift their souls, judiciously,
And save the virtue that survives.

The church, six hundred years ago,
With Michael as its patron saint,
Was built to reach from life below
Toward perfect faith, without restraint.

The builders laid a true foundation
Upon the earth, on solid ground,
So that a later elevation
Was based on footings that were sound.

Design obeyed prevailing rules,
Fulfilling sure and true conviction
That structures might be vestibules
Where we receive God's benediction.

The walls were thin, transmitting light
Through glass that ribs would intersect,
And reaching to a greater height
Than any novice might expect.

Each visitor would feel his eyes
Uplifting to an elevation
Where honor and respect arise
And faith would reach its culmination.

The glass allowed the light within
To circulate throughout that space,
Refracted from its hard and thin
Emergence from some distant place.

Intense and penetrating light
Would reach the windows far above,
And passing through would disunite
And soften into shades of love.

The colored glass was mainly blue,
Transmitting this untroubled shade
To those within, who then withdrew
From any grief their lives displayed.

All those who were within the nave
Could feel release from outer tension,
As inner peacefulness forgave
Their former fear and apprehension.

Not only from this abstract dread
Were rootless lives and souls protected,
The roads to Coventry had led
To shelter from the unexpected.

The church had offered travelers
Six hundred years of sanctuary,
The highest lords, and commoners
Found refuge from an adversary.

This space embedded in a world
Of chaos seemed to be immune
From violence which often swirled
As fiercely as fall leaves are strewn.

But this illusion reached its end
One night with brutal suddenness,
As if pure evil could transcend
The limits virtue might possess.

Like flying horsemen, this apocalypse
Descended from a dark and sullen sky;
The sun was gone, and moonlight in eclipse
Increased its potency to terrify.

The focus of its anarchy, the spire,
Reduced the structure to an empty shell,
As all around, the city was on fire;
Perversion of God's Paradise is Hell.

Some wanted to restore the House of God
In all its purity and Innocence,
As if no evil force had ever trod
Upon the earth in pure malevolence.

Some others would demolish what remained,
Erasing signs there ever was a threat,
Iniquity which could not be explained
Nor understood, one might as well forget.

The wisest knew that evil must be faced,
And memory of devastation mattered,
That past betrayal should not be erased,
And so they left it there in fragments, shattered.

But also knowing that the end of hope
Is not acceptable as life goes on,
They looked for ways in which mankind could cope
And build upon the ash of what was gone.

They therefore raised a new cathedral there,
Not as a surrogate for what was lost,
But as a sign that they were yet aware
That life went on, beyond this holocaust.

The newer nave was higher than the old,
And built so that its western end was facing
The recent ruins that it reached to hold
With arms extended out, as if embracing.

The sum, a synthesis of old and new
Was meant to show that good and evil share
A common ground, but false gives way to true
And life can follow loss, and hope, despair.

Commitment to a new and honest life
Encloses and surpasses former faults,
Deception and betrayal lead to strife
That faithfulness acknowledges and halts.

The lesson was not innocence betrayed,
Nor that a love and faith could be destroyed,
But that survivors must not be afraid
And by their disillusion leave a void.

So love, let us embrace our past
Imperfect as it well may be,
Mistakes there will not be the last
Or worst that we will ever see.

If we ignore our prior flaws
As if they never had arisen,
Enlightened moral growth withdraws
And we remain within their prison.

And should we bury them discretely,
Pretending that if we but cover
Our indiscretions so completely,
They will not harm another lover?

Then we deceive ourselves and others
For none of us are free of faults,
Hypocrisy becomes another's
Mistrust, and thus conviction halts.

So looking back at all the shards
Of faith that I (or others) shattered,
Once rare and priceless, now discards,
I thought of lives in which they mattered.

Remembering the many times
I thought that I had found true feelings
Which all became mere pantomimes
Or, as in games of cards, misdealings.

I found but one, in all the years
That granted failings, paid its dues,
And when I dream of faith appears
As love that I will never lose.

For there are such, though they are rare,
Affections future, present, past,
If you meet one for whom you care,
Protect it well, for it will last.

The heart, embracing its mistakes,
Yet with the dream to rise above
Its weakness shows a strength which makes
It worthy of eternal love.

I REMEMBER

I remember all the days
We spent together since we met,
As if some lingering malaise
Will not allow me to forget.

I still was young, and you were too,
And both were damaged by our past,
But neither recognized or knew
How long the injury would last.

I remember how by chance
I found you were alone as well,
Not searching for a new romance,
But refuge from its carousel.

The revelry of early love
Will circle at a pace unknown
Until one finds the coldness of
The places where one may be thrown.

I remember painted horses
We all would ride when love was new,
They followed ring-shaped circling courses
That led us all, who knew where to?

The carousel revolved around,
And all who rode it were enthralled
With superficial sight and sound,
Until the laughter was recalled.

Then I remember music ceasing,
The gaudy tunes that matched our mood,
The happiness we had been leasing
Foreclosed into disquietude.

The ones who matched remained together,
Or found a newer liaison,
There never was a question whether
The revelry would soon go on.

I remember, it began
Again, much as it had before,
A circulating caravan,
But I was left outside the door.

For one or two were disconnected,
No longer part of any pair,
Nor of the group, and now neglected
No longer fit in anywhere.

I remember those flirtations
Into which I had intruded,
The frivolous and false relations,
From which I found myself excluded.

For one may touch, in innocence
The circle of a certain girl,
But lacking charm and eloquence
Will never penetrate the swirl.

And I remember when I knew
That I could never be a part
Of all her shallow retinue,
Nor find the key that sealed her heart.

For just a minute, music ceased,
The whirligig delayed rotation
And some whose places had been leased
Found these had lost their validation.

But I remember standing there
And watching games once more begin,
They seemed suspended in midair
And colored like a harlequin.

Festivities began once more
And moved together to some place
Where all I had observed before
Continued at a frantic pace.

That was the moment, I recall,
That I first knew that I had changed;
In moving past the carnival,
Priorities were re-arranged.

And I was left, as at a station,
Deserted when its train is gone,
Exhausted from exhilaration
Of superficial goings-on.

I looked for others left behind,
Remembering an even pair
One part of which, now undefined
Might find a new reflection there.

And then I saw someone was waiting
As if she also had forsaken
The revelry and celebrating,
The journey I had undertaken.

Festivities must someday cease
As all of us will soon discover,
The ones who would extend their lease
Will simply find a newer lover.

But there are those who leave the train,
Step off the slowing carousel,
Begin a love they can sustain
And bid the frivolous farewell.

The fortunate are those who find
Another, equally mature,
Who is concurrently inclined
To seek a love that is secure.

And I remember you appeared
Just when I needed re-assurance
That isolation, which I feared,
Could be contained by love's endurance.

I needed you, you came to me,
Both refugees from senseless mirth,
Requiring more security
Than we had found so far on earth.

And I remember well that day
When you said, "Love, let us be true,"
I knew that I was home to stay,
And so I was, with only you.

WHEN I WAS ONE

When I was one and you were one,
The two of us made two,
For love had then not yet begun,
Nor would, for all we knew.

But somehow we grew closer, whether
By chance or by design,
And found ourselves alone together,
With lives that might combine.

And so it was, as time went by
That two became as one,
And what would once diversify
Was now in unison.

I find myself now but one-half,
And you the other part,
One single point upon a graph,
One undivided heart.

Co-ordinates in life will change
And some are bittersweet,
While time itself will rearrange
The challenges we meet.

But even altered lines of force
Must somewhere intersect;
If we together trace their course,
Our lives will there connect.

If we can hold each other tightly
Without a span between,
Though hazards may be present nightly,
Our love will be serene.

And even when the world goes by
And seems to be misguided,
The single space we occupy
Can never be divided.

RESOLUTION

Impulsive loves of youth are never true
But immature young men pretend they are,
And so did I when young, when I, like you
Found passion and delight spectacular.

The vows of youthful love cannot be trusted,
But young girls always dream and think they can,
Conceivably a phase may be adjusted,
Perhaps their lover is a gentleman.

So all of us will find, when we are young
That youthful passion will distort our mind
And each and every love-song that is sung
Forgets, and leaves the future far behind.

The heart that truly loves may someday ache
When placed, a souvenir, upon a shelf,
But each must try, and make its own mistake,
And learn this painful lesson for itself.

And thus we strive, as boats against a current,
To reach a goal that is a fantasy,
We lack, in foolish youth the sole deterrent,
Of wisdom, which we earn through misery.

If early in our lives we were aware
Of what we learn through love and then through loss
We would not venture with so little care
Upon this fragile bridge, and try to cross.

But our illusions show us paradise,
A golden city shining on a hill,
They lure us into foolishness, entice
Us into ventures which prove volatile.

No person who has walked through burning coals
Of disappointment, disillusion, grief
Of love betrayed will still believe in goals
Of ecstasy, which often prove too brief.

It would be better if we all were wise
Before the time when we would be so tempted
That we saw love in such a false disguise
Or if some one of us could be exempted.

But sadly, just a few can see so clearly
The outcome of their youthful love's assurance
That sentiment is infinite (or nearly),
And know that lasting love requires endurance.

So I am glad that when we met, already
We both had passed the stage of youthful folly,
And knew that love, when true, is firm and steady,
Released from rapture and from melancholy.

It matters not the paths that we have taken,
Or how young shallow passion was suppressed,
What is important is that we awaken
Together when our loves can coalesce.

And this has made the difference through time,
For when you are distressed, I am aware,
A shared concern will make a love sublime,
Whenever I may need you, you are there.

This partnership, unlike the loves of youth
Does not depend on passion's sudden flare,
But rather on fidelity and truth,
More comforting than any brief affair.

Devotion such as this requires maturity
And represents continuing endeavor,
But its reward, emotional security,
Will be a blessing which will last forever.

COMMITMENT

No more than once, in everyone's existence
Will come a time of change that is profound,
And only looking back, from some great distance
We see what we have lost, what we have found.
When we were young, as years are young in May,
We lived our lives with energy and passion,
And never dreamed that fate would not obey
Our wishes to continue in this fashion.
But that was not to be, we reached September
And with the coming autumn felt transition,
The vigor of our youth we would remember,
But could no longer reach that past condition;
And only then discerned the value of
Commitment to eternal deep-heart love.

"Dear Memory, preserve her as she used to be.
And Memory, bring back to me tonight all that you can
of this love of mine, all that you can."

from the poems of
Constantine P. Cavafy

"Good-night; ensured release,
Imperishable peace,
Have these for yours,
While sea abides, and land,
And earth's foundations stand
And heaven endures.

When earth's foundations flee
Nor sky nor land nor sea
At all is found;
Content you, let them burn,
It is not your concern;
Sleep on, sleep sound."

from "Last Poems"
A.E. Houseman

Printed in the United States
by Baker & Taylor Publisher Services